Gettysburg

The Complete Pictorial of Battlefield Monuments

By
D. Scott Hartwig
and
Ann Marie Hartwig

THOMAS PUBLICATIONS
Gettysburg PA 17325

This book is humbly dedicated as an additional commemoration in honor of the brave men who lived and served proudly, and often died upon these very fields.

The authors wish to express their appreciation to William Cole of the Eastern National Park and Monument Association for his thoughtfulness and knowledgeable consultation. They also wish to acknowledge G. Douglas Hartwig who made numerous trips between Gettysburg and Philadelphia to aide in the development of this book.

Every effort has been made to provide a photographic record of each monument upon the Gettysburg field of battle. Sometimes this was under disadvantage of heavy foliage, difficult lighting position, or deterioration of the monument. However, the privilege of gathering this material and observing the beauty of these memorials and commemoratives touches the very soul. In many instances the exhibition of this art work is remarkable and we believe that it is worthwhile to find that path and take that extra hike in order to personally experience the love that a country has for its valiant men.

If you persevere you will be rewarded with tender intimacies of these honored men of the Gettysburg battlefield such as the inscription of N.Y. Battery E "...committed to the care of a dear country we were proud to serve."

Table of Contents

1ST ANDREW
SHARP-SHOOTERS,
UNATTACHED MASS. VOL.
IN ACTION
JULY 3RD 4TH & 5TH 1863.
IN DIFFERENT POSITIONS.

——————————

IN GOD WE PUT OUR TRUST,
BUT KEPT OUR POWDER DRY.

The Monuments at Gettysburg

They stand silent and unmoving, yet they speak volumes. They are composed of granite, sandstone, marble, and the like, yet they represent mortal men who stained these fields with their blood. They are the monuments and memorials of the Gettysburg battlefield. Numbering 1,320 all told, they dominate the battlefield landscape, providing mute testimony to the three terrible days in July 1863 that left 51,000 American soldiers dead, wounded, or captured.

The battlefield's extensive monumentation had its antecedents and encouragement in the Gettysburg Battlefield Memorial Association, which was initiated in September 1863 by Gettysburg lawyer David McConaughy. Motivated by an unselfish purpose, shortly after the battle, McConaughy purchased several sections of land that had figured importantly in the fighting with the idea of preserving them as a memorial park. On August 14, 1863, just over a month after the battle, he carried his idea to several of Gettysburg's prominent citizens, proposing that they establish a memorial or monument association dedicated to preserving the battlefield as it appeared in July 1863. This remarkable idea was adopted and in April 1864 the association was chartered under the laws of Pennsylvania, probably the first memorial park to

a battle established during wartime in this country.

It was not until the late 1870s however, that the GBMA (Gettysburg Battlefield Memorial Association) became active in marking and memorializing the field. The impetus for this emerged from the 1878 reunion and battlefield encampment of the Pennsylvania branch of the Grand Army of the Republic, the newly founded, powerful Union veterans organization. During the reunion the Strong Vincent Post of Erie, Pennsylvania, erected a marble marker on Little Round Top to Brigadier General Strong Vincent, who fell mortally wounded in defense of the hill. Philadelphia post #19, a short time later, likewise, placed a small marker in memory of Colonel Fred Taylor, who was killed in command of the 13th Pennsylvania Reserve on July 2nd. The following year, 1879, the survivors of the 2nd Massachusetts infantry erected the first regimental monument on the battlefield at the point where they began their desperate charge across Spangler meadow on July 3rd.

It was during the reunion of the Pennsylvania veterans on the battlefield that the GAR (Grand Army of the Republic) realized the potential of the GBMA and in 1880, the powerful veterans organization gained control of the association's

board of directors. Under its new leadership, the association began to actively encourage other GAR posts and survivor's associations to erect monuments to their units on the battlefield. The veterans responded enthusiastically and by the 25th anniversary of the battle, in 1888, nearly 200 monuments and markers had been placed on the field and in the National Cemetery. The years of 1888 and 1889 were the watershed years of monumentation on the field with upwards of 150 regimental monuments and markers being erected.

Funding for these monuments came from a variety of sources. The state of Ohio, for example appropriated the funds for each of its state unit monuments. In other instances funding came solely from the veterans or was supplemented by assisting funds from their states.

With two exceptions, the monuments were exclusively Union. This was partially due to the location of Gettysburg. Situated in a northern state it was more convenient to northern veterans to visit, and being one of the north's greatest victories in the war, it was only natural that northern veterans would express greater interest in commemorating their deeds there than southern veterans. Depressed economic conditions in the south also contributed to the scarcity of Confederate monuments. Money simply was not available to erect monuments on far away fields like Gettysburg. Lastly, the War Department policy was that regimental monuments should be erected upon its particular army's main line of battle. For the southern regiments this meant where their attacks originated from, not where they had suffered their greatest losses. Consequently, southern veterans displayed little interest in raising monuments at Gettysburg.

On February 11, 1895, Gettysburg National Military Park was established by an act of Congress and the GBMA passed its 522 acres of battlefield land to the administration of the United States War Department. The War Department had been active in the preservation and expansion of the battlefield park since May 1893, when a three man battlefield commission was appointed to administer the expenditure of $50,000 appropriated by Congress to purchase lands, construct avenues, and mark the positions of both armies. The park's establishing law however, provided greater strength to the commission, enabling them to expand the park's boundaries from 522 to 3,874 acres, and to lay out the park in an organized manner, with avenues and narrative tablets marking the positions of combat units of both armies.

Two of the three original War Department commission members were war veterans; chairmen Colonel John P. Nicholson, formally of the 23rd Pennsylvania infantry and Brigadier General William H. Forney, formally of the 10th Alabama infantry. The third member, John B. Bachelder, was a noted historian of the battle.

Between 1893 and 1895, commission members Forney and Bachelder died. Their replacements were Major Charles Richardson, formally of the 126th New York infantry and Major William M. Robbins, formally of the 4th Alabama, and a veteran of the battle. Both men added unique talents and vigorous energy to the commission but Robbins, with his many contacts among ex-Confederate soldiers and his tireless efforts to encourage them to actively assist in the development of the military park, was able to assure that the Confederate army's part in the battle was fully and accurately told.

The accomplishments of this three man commission and their able engineer, E.B. Cope, from 1895 to 1905, when Robbins died, were prodigious. Twenty miles of avenues were completed, defense works were stabilized or rebuilt, over 300 condemned cannon were mounted on cast-iron carriages and placed to mark approximated battery positions, more than 800 acres of land was acquired, cast iron and bronze narrative tablets marking the position and describing the action of every battery, brigade, division, corps, army, and U.S. regular army unit were placed, and the list of accomplishments went on.

Stewardship of the park changed again in 1933, when the administration of the National Cemetery and Military Park was transferred to the National Park Service. In 1938, the Park Service played host to the 75th anniversary of the battle and final reunion of the aged veterans of the blue and gray. The climax of the reunion events was the dedication of the Eternal Peace Light Memorial, which was attended by President Franklin Roosevelt and over 200,000 visitors. When the veterans departed at the reunion's end it marked the passing of an era.

Despite the passing of the veterans, the memorialization of the battlefield continued. Since 1961, eight southern states have erected state memorials honoring their sons who fought at Gettysburg. A regimental marker to the 20th New York Militia was placed in 1981 and two markers commemorating the actions of the Confederate 26th North Carolina infantry have been erected; the most recent in October 1986. An extensive monument restoration program has also been implemented to restore deteriorated monuments to their original condition and beauty. Thus, the memory of the veterans and "what they did here," has not been forgotten, and the work they began, to commemorate their deeds for future generations, will be preserved and continued.

This monument will be a lasting record of your devotion and bravery as long as granite will endure. Future generations will visit this famous field, and gaze with wonder and admiration upon this spot, made sacred by your blood and devotion.

—Oration at the dedication of the 107th New York Infantry Monument

The War Department

The battlefield contains over 200 bronze tablets explaining the participation in the battle of every battery, brigade, division, corps, army, and United States Regular Army regiment. These were prepared by the War Department and their placement on the field was largely completed by 1912. Their text was written by former veterans serving on the Battlefield Commission, like William Robbins and Charles Richardson. These men strove to explain what each unit in the battle did in a straightforward, non-judgmental manner. In this they were successful. The tablets have withstood the test of time and remain an excellent interpretive tool in helping visitors understand the battle.

To further facilitate your understanding of the battle and battlefield of today, it is useful to have an understanding of the size of the various units of both armies that fought the battle. The following table gives average sizes. These could, and did, vary widely from unit to unit in each army.

UNION—ARMY OF THE POTOMAC

Battery—4 guns, 120 men
Regiment—300 - 400 men
Brigade—4 - 5 regiments, 1500 men
Division—2 brigades, 3,000 - 4,000 men
Corps—3 divisions, 10,000 - 13,000 men
Army—7 corps, and 1 cavalry corps, 92,000 men

CONFEDERATE—ARMY OF NORTHERN VIRGINIA

Battery—4 guns, 80 men
Regiment—300 - 400 men
Brigade—4 to 5 regiments, 1,500 men
Division—4 brigades, 6,000 - 8,000 men
Corps—3 divisions, 20,000 men
Army—3 corps and 1 cavalry division 72,000 men

BATTERY

U.S. REGULAR INFANTRY

U.S. BRIGADE

C.S. BRIGADE

DIVISION

CORPS & ARMY

HEADQUARTERS

Equestrian Bronzes

Major General
George G. Meade

Major General
John F. Reynolds

9

Equestrian Bronzes

Major General
Winfield S. Hancock

Major General
John Sedgwick

Major General
Oliver O. Howard

Major General
Henry Slocum

10

Bronze Statues

Brigadier General
Francis C. Barlow

Major General
John Buford

John Burns

Father William Corby

Major General
Abner Doubleday

Brigadier General
John Geary

Brigadier General
George S. Greene

Brigadier General
Alexander Hays

Brigadier General
A. A. Humphreys

Bronze Statues

Major General
John F. Reynolds

Brigadier General
John Robinson

Brigadier General
James Wadsworth

Major General
Gouverneur K. Warren

Brigadier General
Alexander Webb

Major William Wells

Brigadier General
Samuel W. Crawford

Brigadier General
John Gibbon

Confederate State Memorials

Virginia Monument

North Carolina Monument

Mississippi Monument

Confederate State Memorials

Alabama Monument

Florida State Monument

Georgia Memorial

Arkansas Monument

Confederate State Memorials

Louisiana Monument

South Carolina Monument

Tennessee Monument

Texas Monument

Union State Memorials

Pennsylvania Monument

New York Monument

Indiana Monument

New York Auxiliary

Commemorative Monuments

Peace Memorial
North Confederate Avenue
Oak Hill
July 3, 1938

Monument to the United
States Regulars
Hancock Avenue, south of the
Clump of Trees
May 31, 1909

Soldiers' National Monument
National Cemetery
July 1, 1869

Lincoln Speech Memorial
National Cemetery
January 24, 1912

Commemorative Monuments

Soldiers and Sailors of the
Confederacy Memorial
South Confederate Avenue
August 25, 1965

High Water Mark of the
Rebellion Monument
Hancock Avenue, Clump of Trees
June 2, 1892

Kentucky, Marker
National Cemetery
November 19, 1975

Gregg Cavalry Shaft
East Cavalry Field, Gregg Avenue
October 15, 1884

The Regimental Monuments

4TH MICHIGAN INFᵀʳʸ
2ᴺᴰ Bʳᴵᴳ 1ˢᵀ Dᴵᵛ 5ᵀᴴ CORPS.
PARTICIPATED IN 53 SKIRMISHES AND GENERAL ENGAGEMENTS
FROM BULL RUN VA. JULY 21ˢᵀ 1861 TO APPOMATTOX VA. APRIL 9ᵀᴴ 1865

HOW TO LOCATE A REGIMENTAL MONUMENT

This guide is organized with the states listed alphabetically, Union states first, followed by the United States Sharpshooters monuments and the Confederate states. The monuments are listed sequentially, beginning with infantry, followed by cavalry and artillery.

5th Conn. Infantry
Slocum Avenue

14th Conn. Infantry
North Hancock Avenue

14th Conn. Infantry
Bliss Farmhouse Site

17th Conn. Infantry
East Howard Avenue

17th Conn. Infantry
Wainwright Avenue

20th Conn. Infantry
Slocum Avenue

27th Conn. Infantry
Wheatfield

27th Conn. Infantry
Brooke Avenue

27th Conn. Infantry
Rose Grove north of monument

2nd Conn. Artillery
South Hancock Avenue

1st Del. Infantry
North Hancock Avenue

1st Del. Infantry
Bliss Farm Buildings

2nd Del. Infantry
Brooke Avenue

2nd Del. Infantry
North Hancock Avenue

82nd Ill. Infantry
West Howard Avenue

8th Ill. Cavalry
South Reynolds Avenue

8th Ill. Cavalry (Co. E), Marker
Chambersburg Pike &
Knoxlyn Road

12th Ill. Cavalry
North Reynolds Avenue

7th Ind. Infantry
Summit Culp's Hill

14th Ind. Infantry
East Cemetery Hill

19th Ind. Infantry
Meredith Avenue

20th Ind. Infantry
Cross Avenue, Rose Grove

27th Ind. Infantry
Carman Avenue near Rock Creek

27th Ind. Infantry, Marker
Spangler Meadow

3rd Ind. Cavalry
North Reynolds Avenue

3rd Maine Infantry
Peach Orchard

3rd Maine Infantry, Marker
Berdan Avenue, Pitzer Woods

3rd Maine Infantry, Marker
Hancock Avenue

4th Maine Infantry
Devil's Den, Crawford Avenue

4th Maine Infantry, Marker
Hancock Avenue

5th Maine Infantry
South Sedgwick Avenue

6th Maine Infantry
Howe Avenue
east of Big Round Top

7th Maine Infantry
Neill Avenue, Wolf Hill

10th Maine Infantry
Baltimore Pike, McAllister Field

16th Maine Infantry
Doubleday Avenue

16th Maine Infantry, Marker
Doubleday Avenue &
Mummasburg Road

17th Maine Infantry
DeTrobriand Avenue, Wheatfield

17th Maine Infantry, Marker
South Hancock Avenue

19th Maine Infantry
Hancock Avenue

20th Maine Infantry
Wright Avenue, Vincent Spur

20th Maine Infantry
Summit Big Round Top

20th Maine Infantry
(Co. B), Marker
east of monument

1st Maine Cavalry
Hanover Road at
East Cavalry Field

B, 2nd Maine Artillery
Chambersburg Pike,
McPherson Ridge

B, 2nd Maine Artillery
Marker,
National Cemetery

E, 5th Maine Artillery
Slocum Avenue, Stevens Knoll

E, 5th Maine Artillery, Marker
Confederate Avenue
near Seminary

F, 6th Maine Artillery
South Hancock Avenue

1st Md. Infantry
Slocum Avenue near
Spanglers Spring

1st Md. Infantry Eastern Shore
North Slocum Avenue

3rd Md. Infantry
South Slocum Avenue

1st Md. Cavalry
Gregg Avenue, East Cavalry Field

Purnell Legion
Gregg Avenue, East Cavalry Field

Battery A
Powers Hill

1st Mass. Infantry
Emmitsburg Road north of
Sickles Avenue

1st Mass. Infantry, Marker
west of monument

2nd Mass. Infantry
Carman Avenue, Spangler Meadow

7th Mass. Infantry
South Sedgwick Avenue

9th Mass. Infantry
Sykes Avenue north slope of
Big Round Top

10th Mass. Infantry
South Sedgwick Avenue

11th Mass. Infantry
Emmitsburg Road &
Sickles Avenue

12th Mass. Infantry
Doubleday Avenue

12th Mass. Infantry, Marker
Ziegler's Grove

12th Mass. Infantry, Marker
South Hancock Avenue

13th Mass. Infantry
Robinson Avenue

15th Mass. Infantry
Hancock Avenue

16th Mass. Infantry
Emmitsburg Road north of
Klingel Farmhouse

18th Mass. Infantry
Sickles Avenue, the Loop

19th Mass. Infantry
Hancock Avenue

20th Mass. Infantry
Hancock Avenue

22nd Mass. Infantry
Sickles Avenue, the Loop

28th Mass. Infantry
Sickles Avenue, the Loop

32nd Mass. Infantry
Sickles Avenue, the Loop

32nd Mass. Infantry, Marker
Sickles Avenue east of the Loop

33rd Mass. Infantry
Slocum & Wainwright Avenues

37th Mass. Infantry
South Sedgwick Avenue

1st Mass. Cavalry
South Sedgwick Avenue

A, 1st Mass. Artillery
National Cemetery

C, 3rd Mass. Artillery
Field north of Valley of Death

E, 5th Mass. Artillery
Wheatfield Road

9th Mass. Battery
Wheatfield Road

9th Mass. Battery
United States Avenue,
Trostle Farmhouse

9th Mass. Battery
North Hancock Avenue,
Ziegler's Grove

1st Mich. Infantry
Sickles Avenue, the Loop

3rd Mich. Infantry
Peach Orchard

4th Mich. Infantry
DeTrobriand Avenue, Wheatfield

5th Mich. Infantry
Sickles Avenue east of the Loop

7th Mich. Infantry
Hancock Avenue

16th Mich. Infantry
Little Round Top, southwest slope

24th Mich. Infantry
Meredith Avenue,
Reynolds Woods

1st, 5th, 6th, 7th Mich. Cavalry
Custer Avenue, East Cavalry Field
(Custer's)

9th Mich. Battery
South Hancock Avenue

1st Minn. Infantry
South Hancock Avenue

1st Minn. Infantry
Hancock Avenue

1st Minn. Infantry
National Cemetery

2nd N.H. Infantry
Peach Orchard

5th N.H. Infantry
Ayres Avenue, Rose Grove
south of Wheatfield

5th N.H. Infantry, Marker
Sickles Avenue,
south of Wheatfield

12th N.H. Infantry
Emmitsburg Road
north of the Klingel Farmhouse

1st N.H. Artillery
National Cemetery

1st, 2nd, 3rd, 4th, 15th N.J.
(Torbert)
North Sedgwick Avenue

4th N.J. Infantry, Marker
Granite Schoolhouse Road

5th N.J. Infantry
Emmitsburg Road
south of Rogers Farmhouse site

6th N.J. Infantry
Crawford Avenue,
Plum Run Valley

7th N.J. Infantry
Sickles Avenue, Excelsior Field

8th N.J. Infantry
Wheatfield

11th N.J. Infantry
Emmitsburg Road
south of Klingel Farmhouse

12th N.J. Infantry
North Hancock Avenue

12th N.J. Infantry, Marker
Bliss Farm Buildings Site

13th N.J. Infantry
Carman Avenue, McAllister Woods

1st N.J Cavalry
Gregg Avenue, East Cavalry Field

A, 1st N.J. Artillery
South Hancock Avenue

B, 1st N.J. Artillery
Sickles Avenue, Excelsior Field

10th N.Y. Infantry
East of Hancock Avenue,
Leister Farm

15th & 50th N.Y. Engineers
Pleasonton Avenue

39th N.Y. Infantry
Hancock Avenue

39th N.Y. Infantry, Marker
west of South Hancock Avenue

40th N.Y. Infantry
East of Crawford Avenue

41st N.Y. Infantry
Wainwright Avenue

42nd N.Y. Infantry
Hancock Avenue

43rd N.Y. Infantry
Neill Avenue, Wolf Hill

44th & 12th N.Y. Infantry
Little Round Top

45th N.Y. Infantry
West Howard Avenue

45th N.Y. Infantry, Marker
McClean Farm Lane

49th N.Y. Infantry
Neill Avenue, Wolf Hill

52nd N.Y. Infantry
Sickles Avenue, the Loop

54th N.Y. Infantry
Wainwright Avenue

54th N.Y. Infantry, Marker
Rock Creek, east of Barlow Knoll

57th N.Y. Infantry
Sickles Avenue, west of Wheatfield

58th N.Y. Infantry
East Howard Avenue

59th N.Y. Infantry
Hancock Avenue near
Clump of Trees

60th N.Y. Infantry
East of summit Culp's Hill

60th N.Y. Infantry Co. I, Marker
east of summit Culp's Hill

61st N.Y. Infantry
Wheatfield

62nd N.Y. Infantry
Field North of Valley of Death

10th Massachusetts Infantry

74th Pennsylvania Infantry

1st New Jersey Brigade

New York State Monument

Hancock Avenue showing U.S. Regulars and Pennsylvania Monuments

29th Ohio Infantry

Alabama State Memorial

17th Pennsylvania Cavalry

C & F, 1st Pennsylvania Artillery

North Carolina Monument

Virginia State Monument

Soldiers and Sailors of the Confederacy Monument

63rd N.Y. Infantry, Marker
east of Loop

Irish Brigade (63, 69, 88 N.Y.
Infantry) Monument
east of Loop

64th N.Y. Infantry
Brooke Avenue, Rose Grove

65th N.Y. Infantry
North Slocum Avenue

66th N.Y. Infantry
Sickles Avenue, east of the Loop

67th N.Y. Infantry
North Slocum Avenue

68th N.Y. Infantry
Wainwright Avenue

69th N.Y. Infantry, Marker
east of Loop

N.Y. Excelsior Brigade
(70, 71, 72, 73, 74) Monument
Sickles Avenue

73rd N.Y. Infantry
Excelsior Field,
west side of Sickles Avenue

76th N.Y. Infantry
North Reynolds Avenue

76th N.Y. Infantry, Marker
Culp's Hill summit

77th N.Y. Infantry
Power's Hill

78th & 102nd N.Y. Infantry
North Slocum Avenue

80th N.Y. Infantry (20 NYSM)
South Reynolds Avenue

80th N.Y. Infantry, Marker
Hancock Avenue

82nd N.Y. Infantry (2 NYSM)
Hancock Avenue

83rd N.Y. Infantry (9 NYSM)
Doubleday Avenue

84th N.Y. Infantry
(14th Brooklyn),
North Reynolds Avenue

84th N.Y. Infantry
(14th Brooklyn) Marker,
Stone Avenue, McPherson Ridge

84th N.Y. Infantry
(14th Brooklyn), Marker
North Slocum Avenue, Culp's Hill

86th N.Y. Infantry
Sickles Avenue, above Devil's Den

93rd N.Y. Infantry
Taneytown Road,
Meade's Headquarters

94th N.Y. Infantry
Doubleday Avenue

95th N.Y. Infantry
North Reynolds Avenue

95th N.Y. Infantry, Marker
Stone Avenue, McPherson Ridge

95th N.Y. Infantry, Marker
Wadsworth Avenue, Oak Ridge

95th N.Y. Infantry, Marker
Chambersburg Pike,
Confederate Avenue

95th N.Y. Infantry, Marker
Culp's Hill Summit

97th N.Y. Infantry
Doubleday Avenue

104th N.Y. Infantry
Robinson Avenue

107th N.Y. Infantry
Slocum Avenue near
Spangler's Spring

108th N.Y. Infantry
North Hancock Avenue,
Ziegler's Grove

111th N.Y. Infantry
North Hancock Avenue

119th N.Y. Infantry
East Howard Avenue

120th N.Y. Infantry
Sickles Avenue, Klingel Farm

121st N.Y. Infantry
Sykes Avenue,
north slope Little Round Top

122nd N.Y. Infantry
North Slocum Avenue

123rd N.Y. Infantry
South Slocum Avenue, also see
marker east of monument

124th N.Y. Infantry
Sickles Avenue above Devil's Den

124th N.Y. Infantry, Marker
Pleasonton Avenue,
Hummelbaugh Farm

125th N.Y. Infantry
North Hancock Avenue

126th N.Y. Infantry
North Hancock Avenue,
Ziegler's Grove

134th N.Y. Infantry
East Cemetery Hill

134th N.Y. Infantry, Marker
Coster Avenue

136th N.Y. Infantry
Taneytown Road
opposite National Cemetery

137th N.Y. Infantry
North Slocum Avenue

140th N.Y. Infantry
Little Round Top

145th N.Y. Infantry
South Slocum Avenue

146th N.Y. Infantry
Little Round Top

147th N.Y. Infantry
North Reynolds Avenue

147th N.Y. Infantry, Marker
North Slocum Avenue

149th N.Y. Infantry
North Slocum Avenue

150th N.Y. Infantry
North Slocum Avenue

150th N.Y. Infantry, Marker
United States Avenue,
Trostle Farm

154th N.Y. Infantry
Coster Avenue

157th N.Y. Infantry
West Howard Avenue at
Carlisle Road

157th N.Y. Infantry
West Howard Avenue at
Mummasburg Road

157th N.Y. Infantry, Marker
Carlisle Road north of
Howard Avenue

2nd N.Y. Cavalry
Pleasonton Avenue

4th N.Y. Cavalry
Pleasonton Avenue

5th N.Y. Cavalry
South of South Confederate
Avenue, Bushman Woods

6th N.Y. Cavalry
Buford Avenue

8th N.Y. Cavalry
South Reynolds Avenue

9th N.Y. Cavalry
Buford Avenue

10th N.Y. Cavalry
Hanover Road east of
US 15 by-pass

Oneida Independent Co.
Meade's Headquarters

B, 1st N.Y. Artillery
(14th Battery Attached)
Hancock Avenue

C, 1st N.Y. Artillery
South Sedgwick

D, 1st N.Y. Artillery
Wheatfield

G, 1st N.Y. Artillery
Peach Orchard, Emmitsburg Road

G, 1st N.Y. Artillery
South Hancock Avenue

I, 1st N.Y. Artillery
East Cemetery Hill

K, 1st N.Y. Artillery
Hancock Avenue

L, 1st N.Y. Artillery (E Attached)
South Reynolds Avenue

L, 1st N.Y. Artillery
East Cemetery Hill

M, 1st N.Y. Artillery
Power's Hill

1st N.Y. Battery
Hancock Avenue

3rd N.Y. Battery
Taneytown Road south of
National Cemetery

4th N.Y. Battery
Sickles Avenue above Devil's Den

5th N.Y. Battery
National Cemetery

5th N.Y. Battery, Marker
Baltimore Pike at
Evergreen Cemetery

6th N.Y. Battery
Taneytown Road north of
Meade's Headquarters

10th N.Y. Battery
Wheatfield Road

13th N.Y. Battery
West Howard Avenue

15th N.Y. Battery
Wheatfield Road

4th Ohio Infantry
East Cemetery Hill

4th Ohio Infantry, Marker
Emmitsburg Road near Long Lane

5th Ohio Infantry
Geary Avenue, Pardee Field

7th Ohio Infantry
North Slocum Avenue

8th Ohio Infantry
Emmitsburg Road & Long Lane

25th & 75th Ohio Infantry
East Howard Avenue, Barlow Knoll

25th & 75th Ohio Infantry
Wainwright Avenue

29th Ohio Infantry
North Slocum Avenue

55th Ohio Infantry
Taneytown & Emmitsburg Roads

61st Ohio Infantry
West Howard Avenue

66th Ohio Infantry
Culp's Hill summit

73rd Ohio Infantry
Taneytown Road,
National Cemetery Annex

82nd Ohio Infantry
East Howard Avenue

107th Ohio Infantry
East Howard Avenue

1st Ohio Cavalry (Co. A & C)
Taneytown Road
north of Pleasonton Avenue

6th Ohio Cavalry
Taneytown Road
north of Pleasonton Avenue

H, 1st Ohio Artillery
National Cemetery

I, 1st Ohio Artillery
West Howard Avenue

I, 1st Ohio Artillery, Marker
Carlisle Road

K, 1st Ohio Artillery
Carlisle & Lincoln Streets

L, 1st Ohio Artillery
Little Round Top

1st Pa. Reserve
Ayres Avenue, Wheatfield

2nd Pa. Reserve
Ayres Avenue, Wheatfield

5th Pa. Reserve
Big Round Top summit

6th Pa. Reserve
North of Ayres Avenue and
Wheatfield Road

9th Pa. Reserve
Warren Avenue between the
Round Tops

10th Pa. Reserve
Sykes Avenue
between the Round Tops

11th Pa. Reserve
Ayres Avenue, Wheatfield

12th Pa. Reserve
Big Round Top summit

13th Pa. Reserve
Ayres Avenue, Rose Grove

11th Pa. Infantry
Doubleday Avenue

23rd Pa. Infantry
North Slocum Avenue

26th Pa. Infantry
Emmitsburg Road
south of Codori buildings

27th Pa. Infantry
Coster Avenue

27th Pa. Infantry
East Cemetery Hill

28th Pa. Infantry
North Slocum Avenue

28th Pa. Infantry
Rock Creek east of Culp's Hill

29th Pa. Infantry
South Slocum Avenue

29th Pa. Infantry
Near Slocum & Williams Avenues

46th Pa. Infantry
South Slocum Avenue

49th Pa. Infantry
Howe Avenue

53rd Pa. Infantry
Brooke Avenue, Rose Grove

56th Pa. Infantry
North Reynolds Avenue

57th Pa. Infantry
Emmitsburg Road at
Sherfy Farmhouse

61st Pa. Infantry
Neill Avenue, Wolf Hill

62nd Pa. Infantry
DeTrobriand Avenue, Wheatfield

63rd Pa. Infantry
Emmitsburg Road
opposite Peach Orchard

68th Pa. Infantry
Peach Orchard &
Emmitsburg Road

68th Pa. Infantry
Wheatfield Road, Wentz Farm

69th Pa. Infantry
Webb Avenue, the Angle

71st Pa. Infantry
Webb Avenue, the Angle

72nd Pa. Infantry
Webb Avenue, the Angle

73rd Pa. Infantry
East Cemetery Hill

74th Pa. Infantry
West Howard Avenue

75th Pa. Infantry
East Howard Avenue

75th Pa. Infantry
National Cemetery

81st Pa. Infantry
Wheatfield

54

82nd Pa. Infantry
North Slocum Avenue

83rd Pa. Infantry
Little Round Top, south slope

84th Pa. Infantry
Pleasonton Avenue

88th Pa. Infantry
Doubleday Avenue

88th Pa. Infantry, Marker
Ziegler's Grove

88th Pa. Infantry, Marker
Forney Field

88th Pa. Infantry, Marker
South Hancock Avenue

90th Pa. Infantry
Doubleday Avenue

90th Pa. Infantry
Ziegler's Grove

90th Pa. Infantry, Marker
South Hancock Avenue

91st Pa. Infantry
Little Round Top summit

93rd Pa. Infantry
South Sedgwick Avenue

93rd Pa. Infantry
Field north of Valley of Death

95th Pa. Infantry
Wheatfield Road
north of Little Round Top

96th Pa. Infantry
Wheatfield Road
north of Little Round Top

98th Pa. Infantry
Field north of Valley of Death

98th Pa. Infantry
Sykes Avenue
north slope of Little Round Top

99th Pa. Infantry
Sickles Avenue above Devil's Den

99th Pa. Infantry
North Hancock Avenue

102nd Pa. Infantry
Field north of Valley of Death

105th Pa. Infantry
Emmitsburg Road and
United States Avenue

106th Pa. Infantry
Emmitsburg Road,
Codori Farmhouse

106th Pa. Infantry, Marker
East Cemetery Hill

106th Pa. Infantry
Hancock Avenue, Clump of Trees

107th Pa. Infantry
Doubleday Avenue

107th Pa. Infantry, Marker
North Hancock Avenue

109th Pa. Infantry
South Slocum Avenue

110th Pa. Infantry
DeTrobriand Avenue, Wheatfield

111th Pa. Infantry
South Slocum Avenue

114th Pa. Infantry
Emmitsburg Road,
Sherfy Farmhouse

114th Pa. Infantry, Marker
Hancock Avenue

115th Pa. Infantry
DeTrobriand Avenue, Wheatfield

116th Pa. Infantry
Sickles Avenue, the Loop

118th Pa. Infantry
Sickles Avenue, the Loop

118th Pa. Infantry, Marker
Wheatfield Road

118th Pa. Infantry
North slope of Big Round Top

119th Pa. Infantry
Howe Avenue

119th Pa. Infantry
North slope of Big Round Top

121st Pa. Infantry
South Reynolds Avenue

121st Pa. Infantry, Marker
Hancock Avenue

139th Pa. Infantry
Field north of Valley of Death

139th Pa. Infantry, Marker
Sickles Avenue, Excelsior Field

140th Pa. Infantry
Sickles Avenue, the Loop

140th Pa. Infantry
Sickles Avenue, the Loop

141st Pa. Infantry
Wheatfield Road, Peach Orchard

142nd Pa. Infantry
South Reynolds Avenue

143rd Pa. Infantry
Chambersburg Pike &
Reynolds Avenue

143rd Pa. Infantry
Hancock Avenue

145th Pa. Infantry
Brooke Avenue, Rose Grove

147th Pa. Infantry
Geary Avenue, Pardee Field

147th Pa. Infantry
South of Monument,
Geary Avenue

147th Pa. Infantry, Marker
Sykes Avenue,
north slope of Little Round Top

148th Pa. Infantry
Ayres Avenue, Wheatfield

148th Pa. Infantry
South Hancock Avenue

149th Pa. Infantry
Chambersburg Pike,
McPherson Ridge

149th Pa. Infantry, Marker
Hancock Avenue

149th Pa. Infantry, Marker
West Confederate Avenue,
Shultz House

150th Pa. Infantry
Stone Avenue, McPherson Ridge

150th Pa. Infantry
Hancock Avenue

151st Pa. Infantry
South Reynolds Avenue

153rd Pa. Infantry
East Howard Avenue, Barlow Knoll

153rd Pa. Infantry, Marker
Wainwright Avenue

155th Pa. Infantry
Sykes Avenue, Little Round Top

26th Pa. Emergency
Junction of Springs Avenue &
Chambersburg Street

1st Pa. Cavalry
Hancock Avenue

2nd Pa. Cavalry
Leister Farm Field,
old Meade Avenue

3rd Pa. Cavalry
Gregg Avenue, East Cavalry Field

4th Pa. Cavalry
South Hancock Avenue

6th Pa. Cavalry
Emmitsburg Road,
south of Ridge Road

6th Pa. Cavalry
Meade's Headquarters

8th Pa. Cavalry
Pleasonton Avenue

16th Pa. Cavalry
Deardorff Farm, south of Hanover
Road on Highland Avenue

16th Pa. Cavalry
Hanover Road

17th Pa. Cavalry
Buford Avenue &
Mummasburg Road

18th Pa. Cavalry
South Confederate Avenue,
Bushman Woods

21st Pa. Cavalry (Co. B)
Baltimore Pike, McAllister Field

21st Pa. Cavalry (Co. B)
Baltimore Pike, McAllister Field

B, 1st Pa. Artillery
South Reynolds Avenue

B, 1st Pa. Artillery
East Cemetery Hill

B, 1st Pa. Artillery, Marker
East Cemetery Hill

C & F, 1st Pa. Artillery
Thompson's
Peach Orchard

C & F, 1st Pa. Artillery, Hampton's
Peach Orchard, Wheatfield Road

C & F, 1st Pa. Artillery, Hampton's
South Hancock Avenue

E, 1st Pa. Artillery
Power's Hill

E, 1st Pa. Artillery
Culp's Hill summit

F & G, 1st Pa. Artillery
East Cemetery Hill

H, 3rd Pa. Artillery
Hanover Road
east of Hoffman Road

2nd R.I. Infantry
South Sedgwick Avenue

2nd R.I. Infantry, Marker
Emmitsburg Road,
south of Codori buildings

A, 1st R.I. Artillery
North Hancock Avenue

B, 1st R.I. Artillery
Hancock Avenue

B, 1st R.I. Artillery, Marker
Knoll west of Clump of Trees

E, 1st R.I. Artillery
Emmitsburg Road
near Wentz Farm

2, 3, 4, 5, 6th Vt. Infantry
Grant's Brigade
Wright Avenue

12, 13, 14, 15, 16th Vt. Infantry
Stannard's Brigade, Column
Hancock Avenue

13th Vt. Infantry
Hancock Avenue north of column

13th Vt. Infantry, Marker
northeast of column (1st position)

13th Vt. Infantry, Marker
west of column (2nd position)

13th Vt. Infantry, Marker
northwest of column (3rd position)

14th Vt. Infantry
Hancock Avenue, south of column

16th Vt. Infantry
Hancock Avenue, south of column

1st Vt. Cavalry
Slyder Farm,
back lane west of Big Round Top

7th W.V. Infantry
East Cemetery Hill

7th W.V. Infantry, Marker
Wainwright Avenue

7th W.V. Infantry, Marker
north slope East Cemetery Hill

7th W.V. Infantry, Marker
Field north of Meade's
Headquarters

1st W.V. Cavalry
Taneytown Road
north of Pleasonton Avenue

3rd W.V. Cavalry
Buford Avenue

C, 1st W.V. Artillery
National Cemetery

2nd Wisc. Infantry
Meredith Avenue,
Reynolds Woods

2nd Wisc. Infantry, Marker
Slocum Avenue, west Culp's Hill

2nd Wisc. Infantry (Co. F), Marker
Slocum Avenue, west Culp's Hill

3rd Wisc. Infantry
Colgrove Avenue
McAllister's Woods

5th Wisc. Infantry
Howe Avenue

6th Wisc. Infantry
North Reynolds Avenue

6th Wisc. Infantry, Marker
Slocum Avenue west of Culp's Hill

7th Wisc. Infantry
Meredith Avenue,
Reynolds Woods

7th Wisc. Infantry
Slocum Avenue west of Culp's Hill

26th Wisc. Infantry
East Howard Avenue

Andrews, Mass., 1st Company
Hancock Avenue

Andrews, Mass., 1st Company
Marker
Ziegler's Grove

C, I & K, (Mich.), 1st USSS;
B, 2nd USSS
west slope Little Round Top

E, (N.H.), 1st USSS;
F & G, 2nd USSS
South Hancock Avenue

A, B, D & H, (N.Y.), 1st USSS
Pitzer Woods, Berdan Avenue

F, (Vt.), 1st USSS
Pitzer Woods, Berdan Avenue

G, (Wisc.), 1st USSS
Emmitsburg Road, Rogers Site

G, (Wisc.), 1st USSS, Marker
west of monument

Andrews, Mass., 2nd Company
Sickles Avenue, the Loop

Andrews, Mass., 2nd Company
Iron Tablet south slope
Little Round Top

D, (Maine), 2nd USSS
Slyder Lane

E & H, (Vt.), 2nd USSS
Slyder Farmhouse

Confederate States

4th Alabama
South Confederate Avenue

2nd Maryland
Slocum Avenue, South Culp's Hill

2nd Maryland, Advance Marker
Slocum Avenue
near Geary Avenue

26th North Carolina
Meredith Avenue

26th North Carolina
Field north of Webb Avenue

43rd North Carolina
East Confederate Avenue

Texas Brigade
South Confederate Avenue

The Friend to Friend
Masonic Memorial

MARYLAND

Maryland Monument

71